Communities

Living in a Rain Forest

By Joanne Winne

Children's Press

...hing
New ... / Sydney

Photo Credits: Cover © Index Stock Photography, Inc; p. 5 © Jack Fields /Corbis; p. 7 © Dennis Marsico /Corbis; p. 9 © Jack Fields /Photo Researchers, Inc.; pp. 11, 13, 15, 17, 19, 21 © Index Stock Photography, Inc.
Contributing Editor: Jennifer Ceaser
Book Design: Nelson Sa

Visit Children's Press on the Internet at:
http://publishing.grolier.com

Cataloging-in-Publication Data

Winne, Joanne.
   Living in a rain forest / by Joanne Winne.
      p. cm. — (Communities)
   Includes bibliographical references and index.
   Summary: Children describe living in rain forests
in Brazil, Hawaii, and New Caledonia.
   ISBN 0-516-23301-7 (lib. bdg.) — ISBN 0-516-23501-X (pbk.)
   1. Rain forest people—Juvenile literature 2. Rain
forests—Juvenile literature 3. Rain forest ecology—
Juvenile literature [1. Rain forests 2. Rain forest
ecology 3. Ecology] I. Title. II. Series.
GN394.W56 2000   00-029519
306'.08'09152—dc21

Contents

We are sisters.

We live in a **rain forest**
in New Caledonia
(**nu** kal-eh-**doh**-nee-ah).

The rain forest is very green.

It has many trees and plants.

7

This is a Kagu (**kah**-goo) bird.

It lives in the rain forest.

It lives only in New Caledonia.

9

My name is Mateus
(mah-**tay**-us).

I live in a rain forest in
Brazil.

11

A river runs through the rain forest.

You can ride on a boat down the river.

Some trees in the rain forest grow nuts.

The nuts are **Brazil nuts**.

My father looks for nuts in the trees.

15

We are brothers.

We live in Hawaii.

Hawaii has many rain forests.

Palm trees grow all around our house.

Coconuts grow on palm trees.

Coconuts are good to eat.

19

We live near a big **waterfall**.

The water falls from a very high place.

21

New Words

Brazil nuts (breh-**zil nutz**) large nuts that grow on certain trees

coconuts (**koh**-keh-nutz) round fruit with hard shells; they grow on palm trees

palm trees (**pahlm treez**) trees with no branches and many large leaves

rain forest (**rayn for**-ist) a thick, green forest that gets a lot of rain

waterfall (**wah**-ter-fawl) a stream of water that falls from a very high place

To Find Out More

Books
In the Rain Forest
by Maurice Pledger
Silver Dolphin Books

Living in a Rain Forest
by Allan Fowler
Children's Press

Web Site
What's It Like Where You Live?
http://mbgnet.mobot.org/sets/rforest/index.htm
This site tells about different kinds of rain forests.
Find out about plants that grow in rain forests.

Index

About the Author
Joanne Winne taught fourth grade for nine years and currently writes and edits books for children. She lives in Hoboken, New Jersey.

Reading Consultants
Kris Flynn, Coordinator, Small School District Literacy, The San Diego County Office of Education

Shelly Forys, Certified Reading Recovery Specialist, W.J. Zahnow Elementary School, Waterloo, IL

Peggy McNamara, Professor, Bank Street College of Education, Reading and Literacy Program

8/05   9   5/05
12/12   ④
2/17 ⑤⑨ 1/17
4/19   ⑤⑨